THE LOCKED ROOM

VIJAYAN PAMPADY

Every other depressed person who things life is over and they are all alone.

Contents

Foreword

Once it starts you cant escape from it. The word "Depression" is too deep. You may run away but he will pick a truck and follow you. Unless you decide that it wont enter your life you will lock up yourself in the room of depression. How much every light comes to your way, you will not be happy. You will still look forward for something which can never happen.

Preface

I have been through tons of depression cycles in life. The day when I was alone and decided to end my life. The day when whole world pushed me out of the mankind, and day when I was all lonely in the dark road.

1. The Locked room

I slept peacefully
I woke up and ran
searching you!
Where did you go?
Your room was locked
All I knew was to bang my head
Which makes a sound
And you used to open.
My head acted weird
Was that you call pain?
You didn't open door,
Where did you go?
I didn't learn to call your name
I didn't know how to call you
I dont reach the door handle to open
I didn't have friends to search you.
My eyes were blurry,
I couldn see anything
Mom told I m in tears
Where did you go?
I took my toy phone
Pressed where ever I knew
I said "Ha ya ya" as usual
But you didn't reply!

I kept looking at ur photos
I realised it's you
And you are not there with me
Where did you go?
Days passed,
Mom told you are at work
I missed you badly
I didn't know where you are!!
She talked to many
Laughed and smiled,
All I knew was to close my eyes
Where did you go?
She took me out,
I remembered you
Holding my little fingers
While driving with me!
I found someone
Looking like you.
I ran and grabbed his leg
Lifting my little hands!
When will you come back?
Why are you silent?
When will you call me?
Where did you go?
Today she took me out
I saw you coming from back
Didn't wanted to loose the dream
I closed my eyes as usual!!

Many carry me now
Some times I feel it's you
And I close my eyes
Not to loose that beautiful dream!
I won't open my eyes
And loose the dream again
Till I see you again,
Where did you go?

2. The Shoe

Beautiful, elegant, vibrant
They screamed !
Laughed out of joy
Danced with happiness!
I got them name
Fame and proud,
People praised
And all went well!
I protected them
Made sure safe
In the muddy roads
In the dirtiest roads.
Praise turned to complaints
Beauty gave way to dirt
They never realised
Thier feet was safe!
They found new shining ones
beautiful, Vibrant and elegant.
My place shifted
To trash can!
Another cycle started
The circle of life!
Selfish motives
Rule the world!

3. Seed

I found a seed in dark desert
I heard her cry loud and clear,
Looked around for her man
Found him walking with closed ears!
I knew what she cried for
The need for care
The need for attention
The need for protection!
The fields got ploughed
More than what needed
With utmost care, love
And she was sowed!
Planted in my heart
Watered with love!
Leaves grew in all shapes
Watched the new life as it rose!
Flowers bloom from buds on stems,
They are as pretty as precious gems
Took me to a different world
The world of happiness and love!
The day of storms and thunder
Bought him back to my field
He found the precious gems,
The new life and spring!

He took her back
Without telling a word
All flowers and gems
Threw stems in fire!
I lost charm of my garden
Scent of my life
Years of hardwork
All my life!

4. But still

You have everything
Still you own nothing.
You have everyone
But still you have no one!
You are high qualified
Still you feel it's useless.
You have a big house
But still you can't live there!
You have lots of wealth
Still you can't use it.
You have tons of cloths
But still you can't wear them!
You are dead
Still you are alive.
You can talk
But still they can't hear!

5. Start and End

Day starts
Sun shines
Winds breeze
Birds chirp!
Rays show aggression
Winds blow massive
Rains act ferocious
Flood times everywhere!
Sun says good bye
Night stays long
World sleeps at peace
I fight with time!
No day no night
No heat and no cold
No rain no flood
No wind and no rays!
Its just tik tok for me
The only sound I hear
Sometimes musical
Otherwise irritating!
Charge getting over
No one recharges battery,
Only sound disappears
So am I from this world!

6. Hell of Thoughts

Middle of night
No sleep just pain!
If this is not hell
Then what is it?
Middle of dogs
Barking on head
Loud and non stop
Relay or chain?
Life shapes as question mark
Asks itself what is it?
If this is not hell
Then what is it?
You builds palace of life
Place last set of bricks
Falls from top
Leaving no mark of building!
World laughs at you
Dogs around barks at you
If this is not hell
Then what is it?
Loved to get hate
Cared to be neglected
Supported to be opposed
Trusted to distrust!

If this is not hell
Then what is it?

7. The Loyal Dog

She slept peacefully
She laughed happily
She stayed calm
I guarded them!
She roamed around
She never worried
She was at ease
I guarded her home!
Years passed I got old,
My eyes were blurred
Legs were painful to walk
She closed the gates!
I was beaten up
I was thrown out
I was scared
I was hungry!
My friends saw me in street
I waved my tail with love
They laughed at me
And barked with sarcasm!
All I can is to wait
For them to come back
Throw some bread crumbs
For my last supper!

Loyalty never pays back
Even in your old age
Loyalty never helps
Even in your death bed!

8. Sugar Daddy & Eve

Commenced Together
Disparete Momentum
Uncharted target
Spats and squabbles!
Aims converged
Destination set
Pace proportionate
Loved company!
Whirlwind blowed
The man barged in
Milestones shake
Goals dissolved!
Suggar daddy bedelived
Adam sat tight
Eve indoctrinated
Jittery ride over rough terrain.
Hands waved
Took 180 degree turn
Adam bestowed bleeding heart
Eve threw it in no time.
Sugar daddy twitched Eve
They cuddled tight!
Adam walked with shadow
Silent tears rolled down!

9. Lost wings

They were strong
They were roboust
They were well built
They were intense.
They helped her to fly high
See the world from different angle
More positive outlook
They changed her life.
They protected her
From heavy rain
Those cold nights
Numerous hot days.
Then the man came,
He convinced her
To make her more beautiful
Attractive and better life.
He took each feather out
It was painful for her,
He showed her colored feathers
Persuaded her to shed more.
He walked away with all she had
With new colored artificial bird with wings
She limped and hobbled,
She lost her wings forver!!!

10. Be and not Be

When sun disappears
You engulf in darkness
When you need some light
I will be there for you!
You are in middle of storm
No one to rescue
You need some help
I will be there for you!
When you slip down
World walks away
Without pulling you up,
I will be there for you!
When you hate your shadow
When you need a shoulder
To cry your lungs out,
I will be there for you.
When you are happy
Surrounded with people
When you are your own
I wont be there for you!
When you feel comfy
When you feel light
When you are attractive
I won't be there for you!

11. Will it change?

I loved and cared
I talked without a break
I was available all time
I forgot myself.
I thght love can change
Stone hearted people
World will be,
A beautiful place to live!
Nothing will change
Stone be stone
Matter remains same
I was told wrong always!
Life has to move on
With changed perceptions
Untold truth
And lots of questions!

12. My life - My Sun

I waited for you,
Long long hours.
Felt like decades
Never I stopped.
I didn't open eye
With out ur first sight.
I waited for you,
Long long hours.
I felt like a blind
It was dark without you
I didn't open my eyes
I waited for you.
They mocked, laughed
I didn't bother.
I waited for you,
Long long hours.
There was no Color,
It was just black
People loved darkness
I waited for you.
You are my energy
You make me beautiful
You call it a day and night
Without your rays I am null.

There are many moons
And lights they depend
For me you are the only light
Only life for me.

13. Wiping Waves

Loved walking with him
Unknowingly brushing against
Touching his fingers
Drawing on him.
Lived in a fools paradise
Thght he loved the company.
Memories never fade
It will kill you from inside.
Never thght it's easy to walk away,
Without looking back ,
Walking with someone,
Sitting right infront to hurt!!!
Never trust a mirage,
Never cry for someone
Who is not yours,
Love your life!
Waves play hide and seek
They soothe you
Make you comfy
But they are never yours!!!

14. He

He was dejected
beaten up brutally
thrashed, abused
mentally and physically.
He suffered
He kept silent
Thinking it will change
A day will be there.
He cared, he loved
Protected guarded,
And he lived for them
Without breathing for self.
The day he realised
He cried his lungs out
And walked away
As they wanted.
Wishing good for them
For their inner peace
Prosperity and happiness
He submitted his prayers.
Seconds wer like decades
He counted for the change
The wait was useless
Nothing changed!

Time started ticking again
Pendulum swinged like earlier
Only he was forced to change
They were worst than before!
Lessons learnt,
Nobody will change
You accept and move
Till the last day!
Will they realise?
When he breathe last?
When he is not der?
When his body is frozen?

15. The dream

The day is black and white
Searched for Colors
Failed miserably.
Found an elevator
Rushed for it
Pressed it multiple times.
Lift was cruising
Up and down
With out stopping!
Black winning over white
Darkness everywhere
Engulfed in darkness.
Rain and thunderstorms
Loud Screams and fear,
Running without aim!
Sirens crying nonstop
Failing mobile flash light
No place to hide.
Ran for life
Without looking back
No one to rescue.
Buildings faded
Barren land welcomed
No place to hide .

End approaching
Nothing to be done
Just wait and embrace death!

16. Thoughts

I thought you were listening
To every beat of my heart
I'd never say a word
And you would read my world.
The silence screaming louder
And the night growing darker
You have a million reasons not to return
Still the desire to meet does burn.
I always wonder what crosses your mind
Myriad thoughts ,like in a bind.

17. The letter from son

Dear Dad,

I don't no what is day and night.

I don't no when I am hungry or not.

I don't no I should drink water if thirsty.

I don't have WhatsApp or Facebook to spend time.

I don't meet people other than you take me.

I don't have friends apart from the ones you introduced.

All I know are the toys which u got me.

I know when to open my mouth when u feed me.

I know when you put me in my bed I need to sleep.

Above all these I know I just have you and mom.

With Love

Son

18. Easy to say

They told it's ur own
They told to be with him
They told to love him
They told to care him.
We started loving each other
We started walking together
We started thinking alike
We started being together.
Life was with him
No life without him
He even counted,
each of my heartbeats.
Now that he is away
They told not to talk
They told don't bother
They told to forget.
It was easy to say
It was tough to practice.
It was easy to separate
It is tough to unite.
You were in my breathe
You knew my thoughts
Still knowing I miss you
You just ignored me.

19. Dreams

I talked with all my heart,
I loved with all my heart,
I cried with my heart out,
I cared with all my senses.
I opened my eyes
Found no one,
I was all alone
I realised it was a dream.
I wish the dream b true
Dreams r like winds
It just comes and goes
But this wind shattered me
Trying to realise I need to start again.
I asked the dream
Can you be with me
Till I realise it's not real,
He didn't bother.
Asked me to be practical,
Live less intense.
Be matured
And live in senses.

20. Love

Have you ever told your mom you don't like her even if she is dark and not so beautiful?
Have you ever told your kid you don't need him as he or she is not fair or cute?
That's pure love!
Love doesn't come in packages!
Love doesn't come in various Colors!
As it is told
Love is patient, love is kind. It does not envy, it does not boast, it is not proud. It does not dishonor others, it is not self-seeking, it is not easily angered, it keeps no record of wrongs.

Printed by Libri Plureos GmbH in Hamburg,
Germany